About This Book

Title: *Hens and Chicks*

Step: 3

Word Count: 175

Skills in Focus: Digraph ch

Tricky Words: female, chirp, farm, coop, farmers, lay, grow, hatch, hutch, down, safe

Ideas For Using This Book

Before Reading:
- **Comprehension:** Look at the title and cover image together. Ask readers what they know about hens and chicks. What new things do they think they might learn in this book?
- **Accuracy:** Practice saying the tricky words listed on page 1.
- **Phonemic Awareness:** Tell students they will read words with the digraph *ch*. Explain that a digraph is two letters that make one sound. Have students listen as you segment the sounds in the word *chick* (/ch/, /i/, /ck/). Ask students to identify what the word is and what digraph they hear in the word. Then ask readers to point out where the /ch/ sound is heard in the word. Repeat with the word *bench*. Offer other examples that will appear in the book: *chomp, munch, chins, check*.

During Reading:
- Have readers point under each word as they read it.
- **Decoding:** If readers are stuck on a word, help them say each sound and blend the sounds together smoothly. Be sure to point out any /ch/ digraph sounds.
- **Comprehension:** Invite students to talk about what new things they are learning about hens and chicks while reading. What are they learning that they didn't know before?

After Reading:
Discuss the book. Some ideas for questions:
- Have you ever seen a hen or a chick? What did it look like?
- Where are some places that hens and chicks might live?

Hens and Chicks

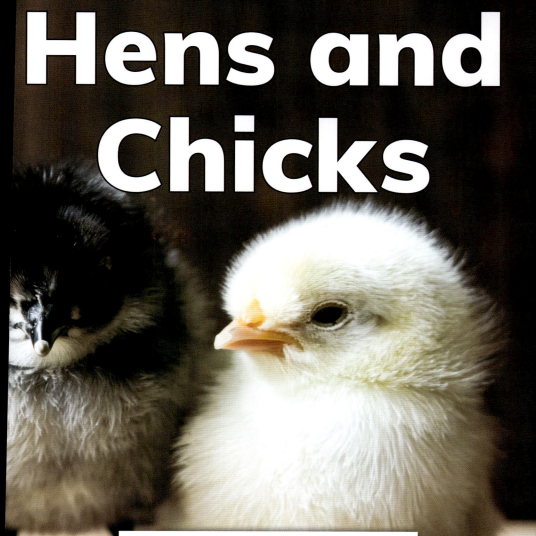

Text by Laura Stickney

Reading Consultant
Deborah MacPhee, PhD
Professor, School of Teaching and Learning
Illinois State University

PICTURE WINDOW BOOKS
a capstone imprint

Hens are female chickens. They chirp and cluck.

Chickens have red flaps of skin on their chins.

Hens are moms. They sit on nests and lay a bunch of eggs. On a farm, the chickens can lay eggs in a coop or hutch.

The hutch has a lock. This keeps chicks and eggs safe.

With no lock, a fox can get in and chomp on the eggs.

Farmers can hunch down and check on the hen's eggs.

They can get a bunch of fresh eggs to cook or sell.

Chicken eggshells are thin. Do not crush or crunch them!

Hens hunch on their eggs. Then the eggs hatch.

Chicks crack out of the eggshells. Chirp!

Chicks have fuzz.
They run and rest.

Hens perch on a bench and check on the chicks.

Farmers feed chicks and hens.

The hens munch and crunch snacks with the chicks.

The chicks shed their fuzz and get big.

Then the chicks grow into big chickens.

Chicks that grow into hens will lay eggs. More chicks will hatch and chirp!

More Ideas:

Phonics and Phonemic Awareness Activity

Practicing Digraph *ch*:
Play I Spy! Prepare word cards with *ch* story words. Place each card face up on a surface. Choose a word to start the game. Break apart the sounds and say, "I spy /ch/, /i/, /ck/" (or another word of your choice). The readers will call out the word, then look for the corresponding card. Continue until all cards have been collected. For an extra challenge, have students be the caller, choosing and breaking apart a word.

Suggested words: chicken, chin, chomp, crunch, bunch, check, bench

Extended Learning Activity

Caring for Chickens:
Ask readers to imagine they are farmers taking care of hens and chicks. Have them think about what the chickens might eat and what they might need to stay safe. Then have readers draw a picture of the chickens in a coop. Ask readers to write a few sentences about their drawing using words with *ch*.

Published by Picture Window Books, an imprint of Capstone
1710 Roe Crest Drive, North Mankato, Minnesota 56003
capstonepub.com

Copyright © 2026 by Capstone.
All rights reserved. No part of this publication may be reproduced in whole or in part, or stored in a retrieval system, or transmitted in any form or by any means, electronic, mechanical, photocopying, recording, or otherwise, without written permission of the publisher.

Library of Congress Cataloging-in-Publication Data is available on the Library of Congress website.

ISBN: 9798875227097 (hardback)
ISBN: 9798875230226 (paperback)
ISBN: 9798875230202 (eBook PDF)

Image Credits: iStock: Akarawut Lohacharoenvanich, 1, 18, alvarez, 10, Capturas E, 12–13, fzant, 2–3, Harlequin129, 8, kivoart, 11, Liudmila Chernetska, 6–7, marieclaudelemay, 17, Oksana_S, 19, phalder, 9, Polawat Klinkulabhirun, 20–21, RyanJLane, 22; Shutterstock: Alter-ego, 14, Majna, cover, Malgorzata Surawska, 15, Oleksandr Lytvynenko, 4, travelwild, 5, 24, Yeasin Arefin, 16

Printed and bound in China. 6274